CW00732050

Bond

STRETCH
Verbal Reasoning
Tests and Papers

9–10 years

Frances Down

Text © Frances Down 2013
Original illustrations © Nelson Thornes Ltd 2013

The right of Frances Down to be identified as author of this work has been asserted by her in accordance with the Copyright, Designs and Patents Act 1988.

All rights reserved. No part of this publication may be reproduced or transmitted in any form or by any means, electronic or mechanical, including photocopy, recording or any information storage and retrieval system, without permission in writing from the publisher or under licence from the Copyright Licensing Agency Limited, of Saffron House, 6–10 Kirby Street, London, EC1N 8TS.

Any person who commits any unauthorised act in relation to this publication may be liable to criminal prosecution and civil claims for damages.

Published in 2013 by:
Nelson Thornes Ltd
Delta Place
27 Bath Road
CHELTENHAM
GL53 7TH
United Kingdom

13 14 15 16 17 / 10 9 8 7 6 5 4 3 2 1

A catalogue record for this book is available from the British Library

ISBN 978 1 4085 1872 4

Page make-up by OKS Prepress, India

Illustrations by OKS Prepress, India

Printed in China by 1010 Printing International Ltd

Introduction

What is Bond?

The Bond *Stretch* series is a new addition to the Bond range of assessment papers, the number one series for the 11+, selective exams and general practice. Bond *Stretch* is carefully designed to challenge above and beyond the level provided in the regular Bond assessment range.

How does this book work?

The book contains two distinct sets of papers, along with full answers and a Progress Chart.

- Focus tests, accompanied by advice and directions, are focused on particular (and age-appropriate) verbal reasoning question types encountered in the 11+ and other exams, but devised at a higher level than the standard *Assessment Papers*. Each Focus test is designed to help raise a child's skills in the question type, as well as offer plenty of practice for the necessary techniques.

- Mixed papers are full-length tests containing a full range of verbal reasoning question types. These are designed to provide rigorous practice for children working at a level higher than that required to pass the 11+ and other verbal reasoning tests.

Full answers are provided for both types of test in the middle of the book.

How much time should the tests take?

The tests are for practice and to reinforce learning, and you may wish to test exam techniques and working to a set time limit. Using the Mixed papers, we would recommend your child spends 40 minutes answering the 65 questions in each paper.

You can reduce the suggested time by five minutes to practise working at speed.

Using the Progress Chart

The Progress Chart can be used to track Focus test and Mixed paper results over time to monitor how well your child is doing and identify any repeated problems in tackling the different question types.

Always read this type of question carefully, as most of them will have similar *and* opposite options.

Underline the two words in each line that are most similar in type or meaning.

Example   <u>dear</u>   pleasant   poor   extravagant   <u>expensive</u>

Take care with words, like 'dear', that have more than one meaning.

1 begin	finish	complete	page	book
2 finger	tow	bell	pull	push
3 spare	room	bath	cooker	extra
4 rainy	fine	cloudy	delicate	clumsy
5 peep	pear	glide	glance	glimmer

○ 5

Find a word that is similar in meaning to the word in capital letters and that rhymes with the second word.

Example   CABLE   tyre   <u>WIRE</u>

6 FOOLISH   lily   _____

7 FIRM   bite   _____

8 CAUTIOUS   dairy   _____

9 SIMPLE   breezy   _____

10 LIFT   gaze   _____

If you cannot find a suitable similar word, try experimenting with rhyming words.

○ 5

Underline the two words, one from each group, that are the most opposite in meaning.

Example   (dawn, <u>early</u>, wake)   (<u>late</u>, stop, sunrise)

11 (gentle, rough, sea)   (wave, sand, calm)

12 (hit, throw, ball)   (thump, catch, stick)

13 (run, slow, fast)   (chase, win, quick)

14 (speak, talk, shout)   (lie, truth, whisper)

○ 4

Underline the two words, one from each group, that are the closest in meaning.

Example (race, shop, <u>start</u>) (finish, <u>begin</u>, end)

15 (afternoon, morning, noon) (midnight, midday, night)

16 (sew, stitch, mend) (break, repair, knit)

17 (gnaw, tooth, fang) (chew, claw, roar) ◯ 3

Underline the pair of words most similar in meaning.

Example come, go <u>roams, wanders</u> fear, fare

> More than one pair of words may have similar meanings. Look for the most appropriate.

18 divide, share multiply, add borrow, steal

19 up, down on, in below, under

20 hair, hare wash, rinse look, find

21 pillow, duvet cushion, chair carpet, rug ◯ 4

Underline the pair of words most opposite in meaning.

Example cup, mug coffee, milk <u>hot, cold</u>

22 clever, intelligent above, below distant, far

23 neither, nor for, four yes, no

24 huge, large immense, minute broad, wide ◯ 3

Underline the word in the brackets closest in meaning to the word in capitals.

Example UNHAPPY (unkind death laughter <u>sad</u> friendly)

25 ODD (out peculiar polite even outside)

26 HIT (miss strike goal punish kiss)

27 SLACK (taut tight quick brief loose) ◯ 3

Underline the one word in brackets that is most opposite in meaning to the word in capitals.

Example WIDE (broad vague long <u>narrow</u> motorway)

28 STRAIGHT (upright even fair forward crooked)

29 CRY (wail laugh pity tear drop)

30 NEAR (close by far there here) ◯ 3

Sorting words

Look at these groups of words.

A	B	C
Animals	Colours	Transport

Make sure you write the correct letter for each answer.

Choose the correct group for each of the words below. Write in the letter.

1–5 blue __   fox __   gerbil __   train __   kiwi __

bus __   turtle __   lorry __   yellow __   pink __

5

Underline the two words that are the odd ones out in the following group of words.

Example   black   <u>king</u>   purple   green   <u>house</u>

6 rose   daisy   sun   garden   daffodil

7 road   lorry   bicycle   car   bridge

8 plunge   lift   fall   tumble   rise

9 Monday   spring   autumn   Tuesday   summer

4

Find and underline the two words that need to change places for each sentence to make sense.

Example   She went to <u>letter</u> the <u>write</u>.

10 The party ended and it was home to go time.

11 The wall jumped gracefully onto the cat.

Always check the sense of the sentence carefully.

12 Please put tidily books away your.

13 The road skidded on the icy car.

4

Fill in the crosswords so that all the given words are included. You have been given one letter as a clue in each crossword.

Use the given letter to place definite words.

14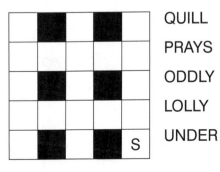

QUILL
PRAYS
ODDLY
LOLLY
UNDER

15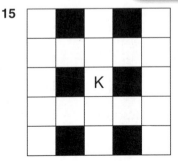

SPACE
CREAM
WAKEN
PEARL
FLAME

6

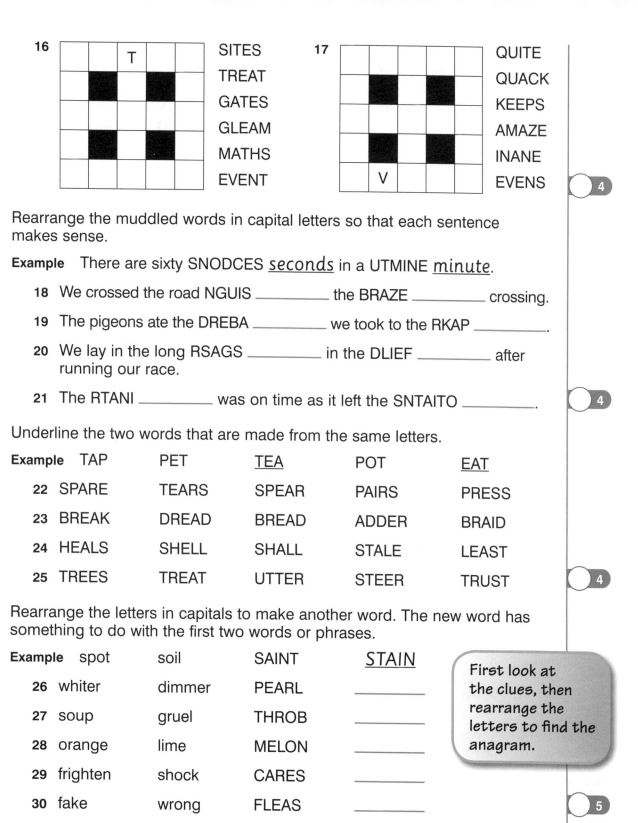

16

		T		
	■		■	
	■		■	

SITES
TREAT
GATES
GLEAM
MATHS
EVENT

17

	■		■	
	■		■	
		V		

QUITE
QUACK
KEEPS
AMAZE
INANE
EVENS

4

Rearrange the muddled words in capital letters so that each sentence makes sense.

Example   There are sixty SNODCES <u>seconds</u> in a UTMINE <u>minute</u>.

18 We crossed the road NGUIS _____ the BRAZE _____ crossing.

19 The pigeons ate the DREBA _____ we took to the RKAP _____.

20 We lay in the long RSAGS _____ in the DLIEF _____ after running our race.

21 The RTANI _____ was on time as it left the SNTAITO _____.

4

Underline the two words that are made from the same letters.

Example   TAP   PET   <u>TEA</u>   POT   <u>EAT</u>

22 SPARE   TEARS   SPEAR   PAIRS   PRESS

23 BREAK   DREAD   BREAD   ADDER   BRAID

24 HEALS   SHELL   SHALL   STALE   LEAST

25 TREES   TREAT   UTTER   STEER   TRUST

4

Rearrange the letters in capitals to make another word. The new word has something to do with the first two words or phrases.

Example   spot   soil   SAINT   <u>STAIN</u>

26 whiter   dimmer   PEARL   _____

27 soup   gruel   THROB   _____

28 orange   lime   MELON   _____

29 frighten   shock   CARES   _____

30 fake   wrong   FLEAS   _____

> First look at the clues, then rearrange the letters to find the anagram.

5

Complete the following sentences by selecting the most sensible word from each group of words given in the brackets. Underline the words selected.

Example   The (<u>children</u>, boxes, foxes) carried the (houses, <u>books</u>, steps) home from the (greengrocer, <u>library</u>, factory).

> Work through, bracket by bracket, and choose the most appropriate words.

1 The (scarecrow, footballer, vegetable) kicked the (can, ball, carrot) from one side of the (table, pitch, kitchen) to the other.

2 (Yesterday, Tomorrow, Next week) it rained and huge (balls, puddles, mirrors) covered the (playground, wall, film).

3 On Mother's (apron, Day, car), my father bought my (dog, brother, mother) a beautiful (book, bunch, crowd) of flowers.

4 She drove her (train, car, boat) down the (road, corridor, slide) and skidded on the (ice, pond, roof).

5 When you mix (blue, red, black) paint with (white, purple, yellow) paint, you make green (porridge, salad, paint).

  5

Choose the word or phrase that makes each sentence true.

Example   A LIBRARY always has (posters, a carpet, <u>books</u>, DVDs, stairs).

6 A LORRY always has (a horn, a driver, wheels, a container, lots of diesel).

7 TOES always have (socks, shoes, a foot, long nails, nail varnish).

8 A DOG always has a (bone, collar, dinner, nose, ball).

9 A SENTENCE always has (pages, chapters, the letter L, paragraphs, words).

10 The SEA always has (boats, fish, water, seaweed, big waves).

  5

Underline the one word in the brackets that will go equally well with both the pairs of words outside the brackets.

Example   rush, attack   cost, fee   (price, hasten, strike, <u>charge</u>, money)

> Often each word in the brackets will go well with one pair of words. Sometimes the answer from the brackets has two very different meanings.

11	paste, glue	twig, wood	(tree, branch, tape, stick, adhere)
12	unripe, young	sickly, unwell	(green, red, black, brown, purple)
13	fib, falsehood	flat, recline	(truth, stand, lie, hide, even)
14	pale, faint	underweight, delicate	(skinny, thin, frail, dark, light)
15	crave, yearn	lengthy, tall	(high, hunger, wish, long, desire)	5

Underline two words, one from each group, that go together to form a new word. The word in the first group always comes first.

Example (hand, <u>green</u>, for)   (light, <u>house</u>, sure)

16	(card, letter, post)	(bell, board, van)
17	(rasp, red, flap)	(door, heart, berry)
18	(king, scare, black)	(crow, crown, row)
19	(shaving, tooth, pick)	(paste, cream, nice)
20	(hear, dirty, play)	(ground, ring, street)	5

> Take one word at a time from the left brackets and put it in front of each of the words in the right brackets.

Underline the one word in each group that **cannot be made** from the letters of the word in capital letters.

Example STATIONERY   stone   tyres   ration   <u>nation</u>   noisy

21	FEATHERS	shear	heath	trash	feast	sheer
22	CURTAINS	stain	trains	saint	trance	strain
23	KITCHENS	chins	stick	chick	kites	thick
24	FOOTBALLS	boots	float	stool	boast	frost
25	NOVEMBER	ember	remove	mover	eleven	venom	5

Underline the one word in each group that **can be made** from the letters of the word in capital letters.

Example CHAMPION camping   notch   peach   cramp   <u>chimp</u>

26	SQUANDER	danger	queer	drain	queen	under
27	MASSAGES	message	games	grass	messes	chasm
28	SCRABBLE	bless	least	bleak	brash	clear
29	POSTMAN	stamen	nasty	spots	stamp	monster
30	FURNACES	creams	scared	surface	crust	snares	5

Focus test 4　Selecting letters

Which one letter can be added to the front of all of these words to make new words?

Example __are　　__at　　　__rate　　　__all　　　　**C**

> Experiment with putting various letters in front of each of the words until you find the correct one.

1 __rifle　　__ape　　__otter　　__ail　　　__

2 __ash　　__hair　　__lip　　__art　　　__

3 __ear　　__lack　　__right　　__less　　　__

4 __eat　　__hoe　　__tile　　__tone　　　__

5 __east　　__end　　__ever　　__adder　　　__

5

Find the letter that will end the first word and start the second word.

Example drow (_n_) ought

6 brus (__) eight

7 foo (__) rail

> Look at the word on the left and find various letters that could finish that word. Then see which one you can also use to start the word on the right.

8 garde (__) ote

9 mimi (__) loser

10 are (__) pples

5

Find the letter that will complete both pairs of words, ending the first word and starting the second. The same letter must be used for both pairs of words.

Example mea (_t_) able　　fi (_t_) ub

11 shin (__) very　　plat (__) ating

12 as (__) eys　　quic (__) ettle

> If you don't succeed with one pair, look at the other pair.

13 lam (__) est　　com (__) ring

14 clif (__) airy　　of (__) amous

15 hurr (__) east　　pla (__) ear

5

Move one letter from the first word and add it to the second word to make two new words.

Example   hunt   sip   <u>hut</u>   <u>snip</u>

> Take one letter at a time from the first word and see if you can make a new word. Then place the letter into the second word until you have made a proper word.

16	dwell	span	_____	_____
17	blame	rave	_____	_____
18	tangle	mean	_____	_____
19	wash	wine	_____	_____
20	stroke	age	_____	_____

5

Add one letter to the word in capital letters to make a new word. The meaning of the new word is given in the clue.

Example   PLAN   simple   <u>PLAIN</u>

21	FOND	discovered	_____
22	YARN	long for	_____
23	CARTON	film made from drawings	_____
24	ANGER	peril	_____
25	BOTHER	a close relation	_____

> Add suitable letters to the word in capitals and think about the meaning to help you. Alternatively, look at the meaning and find a word that uses the word in capitals.

5

Remove one letter from the word in capital letters to leave a new word. The meaning of the new word is given in the clue.

Example   AUNT   an insect   <u>ANT</u>

26	CLIMB	leg or arm	_____
27	CHASE	a container	_____
28	FLOUR	a number	_____
29	FIRST	clenched hand	_____
30	STRING	a bee's weapon	_____

> Here, you need to take a letter away rather than add one.

5

Change one word so that the sentence makes sense. Underline the word you are taking out and write your new word on the line.

Example   I waited in line to buy a <u>book</u> to see the film.   <u>ticket</u>

1 Our cat carried my brother with her sharp claws.   _____

2 My mother plaited my coat as it had grown so long.   _____

3 The referee blew his ball loudly so everyone could hear it.   _____

4 The choir climbed the song tunefully and musically.   _____   **4**

Find the three-letter word that can be added to the letters in capitals to make a new word. The new word will complete the sentence sensibly. Write the three-letter word.

Example   The cat sprang onto the MO.   <u>USE</u>

5 Mary closed the garden G behind her.   _____

6 The queen wore a golden CN covered with jewels.   _____

7 The WHS span on the icy road.   _____

8 When I broke my arm I had to go to HOSAL for an X-ray.   _____   **4**

Find a word that can be put in front of each of the following words to make new, compound words.

Example   cast   fall   ward   pour   <u>down</u>

9 writing	some	cuff	book	_____
10 song	watch	cage	seed	_____
11 land	lighter	way	brow	_____
12 power	work	break	cracker	_____
13 bowl	cake	net	tail	_____

Look for common words such as up/down, black/white, on/in.

5

Change the first word of the third pair in the same way as the other pairs to give a new word.

Example   bind, hind   bare, hare   but, <u>hut</u>

14 tool, too   feel, fee   beer, _____

15 put, pat   bun, ban   fur, _____

See how the letters have been changed and continue the pattern.

16 war, raw   dab, bad   rat, _____

17 stale, ale   flown, own   charm, _____   ◯ 4

Find the four-letter word hidden at the end of one word and the beginning of the next word in each sentence. The order of the letters may not be changed.

Example We had bat<u>s and</u> balls.   *sand*

18 We are going to the cinema later today.   _____

19 I am travelling in this car.   _____

20 The clown made us laugh and laugh.   _____

21 The horse jumped over the gate.   _____   ◯ 4

Look at the first group of three words. The word in the middle has been made from the two other words. Complete the second group of three words in the same way, making a new word in the middle of the group.

Example PAIN INTO TOOK   ALSO SOON ONLY

> Letter by letter, see where the middle word in the first group gets its letters from. Repeat the pattern for the second group of words.

22 CASH SHOP OPEN   PAID _____ LENT

23 HATE HANG SUNG   CLUE _____ WRAP

24 POOR BOOK BEAK   FOUR _____ SLIP

25 WING SING SOCK   PART _____ CLUE ◯ 4

Change the first word into the last word by changing one letter at a time and making a new, different word in the middle.

Example CASE   *CASH*   LASH

26 HARK   _____   WARD

27 POOR   _____   FOUR

28 BEAM   _____   HEAD

29 FISH   _____   WASH

30 MINT   _____   FIST   ◯ 5

> Write down the letters that remain the same. Substitute the remaining letters one at a time.

Now go to the Progress Chart to record your score! Total ◯ 30

If a = 3, b = 2, c = 6, d = 5 and e = 1, find the value of the following calculations.

> Replace the letters with numbers and work out the calculations.

1 c + d = _____

2 a − e = _____

3 c ÷ b = _____

4 a + d + e = _____

5 (b + d) × a = _____

○ **5**

Using the same values, write the answers as a letter.

6 (d + a) − b = _____

7 (ab) ÷ c = _____

○ **2**

If e = 3, l = 1, m = 4, i = 2 and s = 7, what are the totals of these words?

8 lies _____

9 lime _____

10 smile _____

○ **3**

Read the first two statements and then underline one of the four options below that must be true.

11 Her pencils are sharp. All of her pencils are red.

   A My pencil is blunt.

   B All her red pencils are sharp.

   C All pencils in the world are sharp.

   D Red pencils are always sharp.

12 Some houses are made of bricks. All houses have roofs.

   A Houses are not made of stone.

   B Some houses have chimneys.

   C We have a wooden front door.

   D Brick houses have roofs.

○ **2**

Four friends, A, B, C, and D, like different colours. C and D like red. The other two like yellow. A and D like green. B's favourite colour is yellow but she dislikes red. All of them like blue except D.

13 Which is the most popular colour? _____

14 Who likes red as well as green? _____

15 Who likes three colours? _____

○ **3**

LEEDS   HUDDERSFIELD   CROYDON   YORK   READING

If these towns are put into alphabetical order, which comes:

16 first? _____

17 last? _____

18 fourth? _____

> Write the words in alphabetical order before you begin.

A B C D E F G H I J K L M N O P Q R S T U V W X Y Z

If the days of the week are put into alphabetical order, which comes:

19 first? _____

20 last? _____

5

This is a diagram of six school lockers. A and E have already been taken.

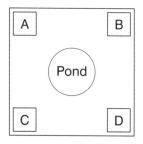

TOP

LEFT   BOTTOM   RIGHT

Write down the children's names. Read each sentence carefully and write down, next to their names, who has which locker using the given information.

Mo took a locker on the top level. Angie took one on the bottom level but not directly under Mo's. Fern's was somewhere to the left of Greg's. He was on the same level as Mo. Which locker did each child take?

21 Mo _____   **22** Fern _____   **23** Angie _____   **24** Greg _____

4

Using the picture below, select the correct compass points in the questions.

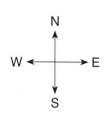

Use the compass points to help you.

25 House A is to the (west, north, east) of House B. _____

26 House D is to the (east, north, south) of House B. _____

27 The pond is (south-west, south-east, north-west) of House A. _____

3

May is four years younger than her sister, Bess, who in turn is twice her little brother, Tom's, age. Sarah, their mother, was 26 when May was born. She is now 32. How old are the children?

28 May _____   **29** Bess _____   **30** Tom _____

3

Now go to the Progress Chart to record your score!   Total   30

The code for CREAMS is 4 8 0 2 9 5. Encode each of these words using the same code.

First line up the code with the word:　　　C R E A M S
　　　　　　　　　　　　　　　　　　4 8 0 2 9 5

Then substitute the letters for numbers.

1 RACE _____　　　　　　**2** SAME _____

Decode these words using the same code as above.

3 5 0 0 9 _____　　　　　　**4** 2 8 0 2 _____

4

The code for STABLE is ← ↓ → ↘ ↕ ↑. Encode each of these words using the same code.

5 BALE _____　　　　　　**6** SALT _____

Decode these words using the same code as above.

7 ↕ → ← ↓ _____　　　　　　**8** → ↘ ↕ ↑ _____

4

Match the right word to each code given below.

　　PLAY　YARD　PEEL　LEAP

Look for letters that stand out. Here, two words begin with P, and one word has a double E.

9 w k z o _____　　　　　　**10** s m k u _____

11 u m m s _____　　　　　　**12** u s k w _____

13 Using the same code, decode z m k s. _____

5

14 If the code for HOLLOW is 4 9 6 6 9 2, what is the code for WOOL? _____

15 Using the same code, decode 4 9 2 6. _____

16 If the code for SPEARS is ? & % @ ! ?, encode PASS. _____

17 Using the same code, decode & % @ !. _____

18 If the code for STRING is F X Z B V O, encode GRIN. _____

19 Using the same code, decode X B V F. _____

Make sure you write down the code accurately.

20 If the code for FASTER is B c 5 k ^ /, what is the code for STAR? _____

21 Using the same code, decode B ^ c /. _____ ⊙ 8

A B C D E F G H I J K L M N O P Q R S T U V W X Y Z

Example If the code for CAT is D B U, what is the code for DOG? <u>E P H</u>

Look at the relationship of each of the letters with its code. Here, the code for C is D, the next letter in the alphabet. Check that the others follow the same pattern.

22 If the code for DESK is E F T L, what is the code for FAME? _____

23 If the code for LEFT is M F G U, what is the code for BARN? _____

24 If the code for BITE is A H S D, what is the code for LOOK? _____

25 If the code for NOTE is M N S D, what is the code for WILD? _____

26 If the code for COMB is E Q O D, what is the code for HAIR? _____

27 If the code for FORK is G P S L, what is T P J M? _____

28 If the code for SAIL is T B J M, what is Q P S U? _____

29 If the code for DUST is C T R S, what is E H Q L? _____

30 If the code for BEAR is D G C T, what is E W D U? _____ ⊙ 9

Complete the following sentences in the best way by choosing one word from each set of brackets.

Example Tall is to (tree, <u>short</u>, colour) as narrow is to (thin, white, <u>wide</u>).

> Look for the relationship between the pairs of statements. Here it is opposites. The second pairing must be completed in the same way.
>
> Look carefully as sometimes there appears to be more than one answer.

1 High is to low as (big, cool, behind) is to (small, dirty, blue).

2 Dog is to (collar, bone, paw) as (horse, bird, lion) is to hoof.

3 Smile is to (toes, mouth, arm) as listen is to (ears, heart, fingers).

4 (Bed, garden, tractor) is to (window, water, pillow) as chair is to cushion.

5 Head is to (brains, hat, hair) as (foot, toenail, nose) is to sock.

6 (Hard, Easy, Moving) is to difficult as (wide, upset, throw) is to broad.

6

Fill in the missing letters. The alphabet has been written out to help you.

A B C D E F G H I J K L M N O P Q R S T U V W X Y Z

Example AB is to CD as PQ is to <u>RS</u>.

> Look for the pattern. In these, both letters are working together.
>
> (It may help to put your finger on the alphabet line and count the number of spaces.)

7 QR is to ST as UV is to ___.

8 VW is to XY as KL is to ___.

9 AC is to EG as NP is to ___.

10 DE is to EF as FG is to ___.

11 ZY is to XW as VU is to ___.

12 AA is to DD as GG is to ___.

6

Give the two missing pairs of letters in the following sequences. The alphabet has been written out for you.

A B C D E F G H I J K L M N O P Q R S T U V W X Y Z

Example CQ   DP   EQ   FP   <u>GQ</u>   <u>HP</u>

> See whether the letters are working together or independently, as in the example.

13	EF	GH	___	___	MN	
14	Zy	___	Vu	Ts	___	
15	___	EG	IK	MO	___	
16	XF	YG	XH	___	___	YK
17	BI	___	___	EL	FM	GN
18	___	KE	LD	___	NB	OA
19	ZB	YD	___	WH	VJ	___
20	Hi3	Jk4	Lm5	No6	___	___

8

Example RS   TU   VW   XY   <u>ZA</u>   <u>BC</u>

> When you reach the end of the alphabet, treat it like a continuous line – XYZAB and BAZYX, and so on.

21	UV	WX	___	___	CD	EF
22	___	CB	___	YX	WV	UT
23	YZ	SA	___	___	YD	SE

3

Give the two missing numbers in the following sequences.

Example 2   4   6   8   <u>10</u>   <u>12</u>

24	24	21	___	15	12	___
25	___	___	27	37	47	57
26	1	5	___	13	___	21
27	55	45	35	___	___	5
28	2	___	8	___	32	64
29	66	3	66	4	___	___
30	3	4	6	9	___	___

> Look for the pattern between the numbers.

> Sometimes, the increase/decrease is irregular.

7

Now go to the Progress Chart to record your score!   Total **30**

19

Mixed paper 1

Underline the two words in each line that are most similar in type or meaning.

Example <u>dear</u>   pleasant   poor   extravagant   <u>expensive</u>

  1 flat   palace   level   heavy   light

  2 grin   mutter   shout   frown   mumble

  3 calm   boil   shiny   bright   sad

  4 distant   near   far   way   view

  5 sun   wind   carve   twist   meat

5

Underline the one word in each group that **can be made** from the letters of the word in capital letters.

Example CHAMPION   camping   notch   peach   cramp   <u>chimp</u>

  6 CRINKLES   chick   skirt   links   crack   scale

  7 BRAVERY   zebra   berry   every   slave   really

  8 CURIOUS   scour   curry   riots   sauce   sorry

  9 MURDERS   dress   drums   medal   rudder   summer

  10 PITCHES   stitch   cheese   cheap   clips   spice

5

Look at these groups of words.

A	B	C
Animals	Stationery	Rooms

Choose the correct group for each of the words below. Write in the letter.

11–15 horse ___   rubber ___   pencil ___   kitchen ___   rabbit ___

         wolf ___   sharpener ___   bathroom ___   cheetah ___   bedroom ___

5

20

Change one word so that the sentence makes sense. Underline the word you are taking out and write your new word on the line.

Example   I waited in line to buy a <u>book</u> to see the film.   *ticket*

16   During the night, clouds fell and our garden was white.   _____

17   At the restaurant, the waiter opened a box of wine
with the corkscrew.   _____

18   Sam gave his cat a bone after taking him for a walk
in the park.   _____

19   The television rang and my mother answered it.   _____

20   A robin is a garden gnome with a red breast.   _____   **5**

Find the letter that will end the first word and start the second word.

Example   drow (<u>n</u>) ought

21   biscui (__) erm   22   donke (__) ard

23   lan (__) ragon   24   pil (__) nough

25   clif (__) orest   **5**

Match the right word to each code given below.

FLAP   FOOL   FLAN   OPEN

26 8 6 6 9   _____   27 6 7 4 3   _____

28 8 9 1 3   _____   29 8 9 1 7   _____

30   Using the same code, decode 7 1 3 4.   _____   **5**

Find the three-letter word that can be added to the letters in capitals to make a new word. The new word will complete the sentence sensibly. Write the three-letter word.

Example   The cat sprang onto the MO.   <u>USE</u>

31   Do up all the TONS on your shirt.   _____

32   Headlines in SPAPERS are usually in capitals.   _____

33   Cars travel on roads, people walk on PAVETS.   _____

34   Edinburgh is the capital of SCOTL.   _____

35   The grass on our garden N needs mowing.   _____   **5**

Add one letter to the word in capital letters to make a new word. The meaning of the new word is given in the clue.

Example PLAN   simple   <u>PLAIN</u>

36 PUMP   fat   _____

37 HAIR   a seat   _____

38 STUCK   hit   _____

39 TART   begin   _____

40 LEVER   intelligent   _____

5

Underline the two words, one from each group, that are the most opposite in meaning.

Example (dawn, <u>early</u>, wake)   (<u>late</u>, stop, sunrise)

41 (rain, storm, wet)   (damp, dry, thunder)

42 (black, biscuit, chair)   (cookie, white, table)

43 (angry, hit, laugh)   (happy, yearn, miss)

44 (smart, brave, bold)   (tiny, even, scruffy)

45 (hurry, talk, warm)   (speak, rush, cool)

5

Underline the two words that are the odd ones out in the following group of words.

Example black   <u>king</u>   purple   green   <u>house</u>

46 sparrow   fox   blackbird   pigeon   rat

47 pencil   pen   crayon   case   card

48 denim   cotton   linen   dress   sweater

49 apple   box   banana   can   orange

50 branch   material   twig   trunk   beetle

5

If a = 1, b = 5, c = 3, d = 2 and e = 10, work out the answers to these. Write your answer as a number.

51 e − (b + c) = _____

52 bc + a = _____

53 c + b + d + a = _____

54 e ÷ d = _____

55 (e + b) − (d + a) = _____

5

Complete the following sentences in the best way by choosing one word from each set of brackets.

Example Tall is to (tree, <u>short</u>, colour) as narrow is to (thin, white, <u>wide</u>).

56 Coffee is to (bean, mug, break) as (water, looking, hall) is to glass.

57 Book is to (read, page, title) as television is to (ring, call, watch).

58 Hot is to (cold, tap, bath) as (unkind, calm, kind) is to cruel.

59 Finger is to (toe, nail, glove) as foot is to (trousers, leg, hand).

60 (Climb, Fast, Back) is to slow as bad is to (good, wicked, hard).

5

Underline two words, one from each group, that go together to form a new word. The word in the first group always comes first.

Example (hand, <u>green</u>, for)   (light, <u>house</u>, sure)

61 (break, mend, still)   (age, term, bottle)

62 (news, garden, avail)   (gate, able, town)

63 (dark, light, big)   (night, noon, house)

64 (pink, high, grape)   (lights, hill, bag)

65 (two, ten, nine)   (lives, or, time)

5

Mixed paper 2

Fill in the crosswords so that all the given words are included. You have been given one letter as a clue in each crossword.

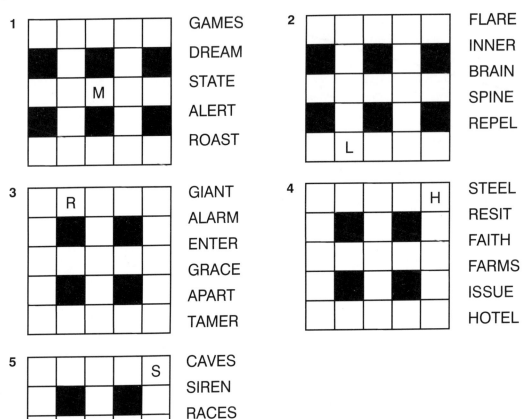

1   GAMES
     DREAM
     STATE
     ALERT
     ROAST

2   FLARE
     INNER
     BRAIN
     SPINE
     REPEL

3   GIANT
     ALARM
     ENTER
     GRACE
     APART
     TAMER

4   STEEL
     RESIT
     FAITH
     FARMS
     ISSUE
     HOTEL

5   CAVES
     SIREN
     RACES
     RARER
     RISEN
     RIVER

Find a word that is similar in meaning to the word in capital letters and that rhymes with the second word.

Example	CABLE	tyre	*WIRE*
6	JUMP	sleep	_____
7	GROUND	birth	_____
8	WEALTHY	ditch	_____
9	IMITATE	sloppy	_____
10	PRIOR	floor	_____

5

5

Complete the following sentences by selecting the most sensible word from each group of words given in the brackets. Underline the words selected.

Example The (<u>children</u>, boxes, foxes) carried the (houses, <u>books</u>, steps) home from the (greengrocer, <u>library</u>, factory).

11 We had (children, computers, sausages), (flowers, chips, moles) and (boats, beans, books) for school lunch today.

12 (Two, Sixty, Forty-four) plus (six, ten, three) equals (five, four, three).

13 My reading (arm, book, station) has one hundred (ants, currants, pages) and it is really (exciting, chilly, damp).

14 We have a nest of baby (elephants, birds, dinosaurs) in our (lorry, fireworks, garden) hedge that the parents are constantly (talking, beating, feeding).

15 We have recycling (bins, balloons, ponds) at the back of the (playground, sky, stool) at (ceiling, school, the sea).

5

Find the letter that will complete both pairs of words, ending the first word and starting the second. The same letter must be used for both pairs of words.

Example mea (<u>t</u>) able   fi (<u>t</u>) ub

16 crac (__) ing   stoc (__) ipper

17 ro (__) erry   cra (__) ox

18 stra (__) et   willo (__) ant

19 baske (__) op   kni (__) error

20 hai (__) et   cal (__) emon

5

GREEN   GREY   RED   BLUE   YELLOW

If these colours are put into alphabetical order, which comes:

21 second? _____

22 third?   _____

23 fourth? _____

3

25

Read the first two statements and then underline one of the four options below that must be true.

24 Beetles are insects. Some beetles have wings.

   A All beetles are insects.   **B** All beetles have wings.

   C Winged insects bite.   **D** All insects are beetles.

25 James is a boy's name. All boys have names.

   A All boys are called James.   **B** James is a girl's name.

   C Every boy has a brother called James.   **D** Some boys are called James.

      2

If the code for PARENTS is □ ÷ ◊ ⌂ ○ ● △, decode:

26 □ ⌂ ÷ ◊ _____   **27** ● ◊ ÷ □ _____

28 △ ● ÷ ◊ _____   **29** ○ ⌂ △ ● _____

30 ● ◊ ⌂ ⌂ _____

      5

Find a word that can be put in front of each of the following words to make new, compound words.

Example	cast	fall	ward	pour	<u>down</u>
31	stairs	stream	hill	on	_____
32	hear	grown	board	night	_____
33	berry	board	bird	currant	_____
34	ball	drop	flake	plough	_____
35	fall	colour	ski	proof	_____

      5

Move one letter from the first word and add it to the second word to make two new words.

Example	hunt	sip	<u>hut</u>	<u>snip</u>
36	brain	ramble	_____	_____
37	glove	ate	_____	_____
38	there	sick	_____	_____
39	grown	fill	_____	_____
40	trickle	spot	_____	_____

      5

Focus test 1

1	finish	complete
2	tow	pull
3	spare	extra
4	fine	delicate
5	peep	glance
6	SILLY	
7	TIGHT	
8	WARY	
9	EASY	
10	RAISE	
11	rough	calm
12	throw	catch
13	slow	quick
14	shout	whisper
15	noon	midday
16	mend	repair
17	gnaw	chew
18	divide, share	
19	below, under	
20	wash, rinse	
21	carpet, rug	
22	above, below	
23	yes, no	
24	immense, minute	
25	peculiar	
26	strike	
27	loose	
28	crooked	
29	laugh	
30	far	

Focus test 2

1–5 blue B; fox A; gerbil A; train C; kiwi A; bus C; turtle A; lorry C; yellow B; pink B

6	sun	garden
7	road	bridge
8	lift	rise
9	Monday	Tuesday
10	home	time
11	wall	cat
12	tidily	your
13	road	car

14

Q		O		P
U	N	D	E	R
I		D		A
L	O	L	L	Y
L		Y		S

15

S		W		F
P	E	A	R	L
A		K		A
C	R	E	A	M
E		N		E

16

G	A	T	E	S
L		R		I
E	V	E	N	T
A		A		E
M	A	T	H	S

17

Q	U	A	C	K
U		M		E
I	N	A	N	E
T		Z		P
E	V	E	N	S

18	using	zebra
19	bread	park
20	grass	field
21	train	station
22	SPARE	SPEAR
23	DREAD	ADDER
24	STALE	LEAST
25	TREES	STEER
26	PALER	
27	BROTH	
28	LEMON	
29	SCARE	
30	FALSE	

Focus test 3

1	footballer	ball pitch
2	Yesterday	puddles playground
3	Day	mother bunch
4	car	road ice
5	blue	yellow paint
6	wheels	
7	a foot	
8	nose	
9	words	
10	water	
11	stick	
12	green	
13	lie	
14	light	
15	long	
16	cardboard	
17	raspberry	
18	scarecrow	
19	toothpaste	
20	playground	
21	heath	
22	trance	
23	chick	
24	frost	
25	eleven	
26	under	
27	games	
28	clear	
29	stamp	
30	surface	

Focus test 4

1	t	
2	c	
3	b	
4	s	
5	l	
6	h	
7	t	
8	n	
9	c	
10	a	
11	e	
12	k	
13	b	
14	f	
15	y	
16	dell	spawn
17	lame	brave
18	angle	meant
19	was	whine
20	stoke	rage
21	FOUND	
22	YEARN	
23	CARTOON	
24	DANGER	
25	BROTHER	
26	LIMB	
27	CASE	
28	FOUR	
29	FIST	
30	STING	

Focus test 5

1	carried	scratched
2	coat	hair
3	ball	whistle
4	climbed	sang
5	ATE	
6	ROW	
7	EEL	
8	PIT	
9	hand	
10	bird	
11	high	
12	fire	
13	fish	
14	bee	
15	far	
16	tar	
17	arm	
18	Wear	
19	scar	
20	hand	
21	dove	
22	IDLE	
23	CLAP	
24	SOUP	
25	CART	
26	HARD	
27	POUR	
28	BEAD	
29	WISH	
30	MIST	

Focus test 6

1	11
2	2
3	3
4	9
5	21
6	c
7	e
8	13
9	10
10	17
11	B
12	D
13	blue
14	D
15	A
16	CROYDON
17	YORK
18	READING
19	Friday
20	Wednesday
21	B
22	D
23	F
24	C
25	west
26	south
27	south-east
28	6
29	10
30	5

Focus test 7

1	8240
2	5290
3	SEEM
4	AREA
5	↘→↕↑
6	←→↕↓

Bond STRETCH Verbal Reasoning Tests and Papers 9–10 years

7 LAST
8 ABLE
9 YARD
10 LEAP
11 PEEL
12 PLAY
13 REAL
14 2 9 9 6
15 HOWL
16 & @ ? ?
17 PEAR
18 O Z B V
19 TINS
20 5 k c /
21 FEAR
22 G B N F
23 C B S O
24 K N N J
25 V H K C
26 J C K T
27 SOIL
28 PORT
29 FIRM
30 CUBS

Focus test 8

1	big	small
2	paw	horse
3	mouth	ears
4	Bed	pillow
5	hat	foot
6	Hard	wide
7	WX	
8	MN	
9	RT	
10	GH	
11	TS	
12	JJ	
13	IJ	KL
14	Xw	Rq
15	AC	QS
16	YI	XJ
17	CJ	DK
18	JF	MC
19	XF	UL
20	Pq7	Rs8
21	YZ	AB
22	ED	AZ
23	YB	SC
24	18	9
25	7	17
26	9	17
27	25	15
28	4	16
29	66	5
30	13	18

Mixed paper 1

1	flat	level
2	mutter	mumble
3	shiny	bright
4	distant	far
5	wind	twist
6	links	
7	berry	
8	scour	
9	drums	
10	spice	

11–15 horse A; rubber B;
pencil B; kitchen C;
rabbit A; wolf A
sharpener B;
bathroom C;
cheetah A;
bedroom C

16	clouds	snow
17	box	bottle
18	cat	dog
19	television	telephone
20	gnome	bird
21	t	
22	y	
23	d	
24	e	
25	f	
26	FOOL	
27	OPEN	
28	FLAN	
29	FLAP	
30	PANE	
31	BUT	
32	NEW	
33	MEN	
34	AND	
35	LAW	
36	PLUMP	
37	CHAIR	
38	STRUCK	
39	START	
40	CLEVER	
41	wet	dry
42	black	white
43	hit	miss
44	smart	scruffy
45	warm	cool
46	fox	rat
47	case	card
48	dress	sweater
49	box	can
50	material	beetle
51	2	
52	16	
53	11	
54	5	
55	12	
56	mug	water
57	read	watch
58	cold	kind
59	toe	hand
60	Fast	good
61	breakage	
62	available	
63	lighthouse	
64	highlights	
65	tenor	

Mixed paper 2

1

D	R	E	A	M
	O		L	
G	A	M	E	S
	S		R	
S	T	A	T	E

2

B	R	A	I	N
	E		N	
S	P	I	N	E
	E		E	
F	L	A	R	E

3

G	R	A	C	E
I		L		N
A	P	A	R	T
N		R		E
T	A	M	E	R

4

F	A	I	T	H
A		S		O
R	E	S	I	T
M		U		E
S	T	E	E	L

5

R	A	C	E	S
A		A		I
R	I	V	E	R
E		E		E
R	I	S	E	N

6 LEAP
7 EARTH
8 RICH
9 COPY
10 BEFORE
11 sausages chips
beans
12 Two three
five
13 book pages
exciting
14 birds garden
feeding
15 bins
playground
school
16 k
17 b
18 w
19 t
20 l
21 GREEN
22 GREY
23 RED
24 A
25 D
26 PEAR
27 TRAP
28 STAR
29 NEST
30 TREE
31 up
32 over
33 black
34 snow
35 water
36 rain bramble
37 love gate
38 here stick
39 gown frill
40 tickle sport
41 9 7
42 5 25
43 15 3
44 12 22
45 11 16
46 before, after
47 careful, careless
48 healthy, ill
49 quickly, slowly
50 inside, outside
51 morning raining
52 bear dog
53 table flowers
54 garage car
55 sky cloud
56 an engine
57 pages
58 surrounded by water
59 feathers
60 heat
61 hat
62 cook
63 bus
64 will
65 one

Mixed paper 3

1 LASS
2 BEST

Bond STRETCH Verbal Reasoning Tests and Papers 9–10 years

3	5 8 3 2		
4	2 8 1 5		
5	LABEL		
6	stamp		
7	wing		
8	iron		
9	star		
10	over		
11	laugh	cry	
12	find	lose	
13	joy	grief	
14	dull	bright	
15	higher	lower	
16	h		
17	r		
18	t		
19	b		
20	s		
21	PR		
22	OW		
23	WX		
24	PU		
25	DW		
26	8		
27	3		
28	6		
29	5		
30	2		
31	bean		
32	slit		
33	tall		
34	they		
35	verb		
36	CHEAP		
37	STEAM		
38	CRATE		
39	TEACH		
40	CHARM		
41	PAST		
42	DEAD		
43	CLAP		
44	EVER		
45	FOND		
46	caught	fell	
47	presents	medals	
48	table	egg	
49	mats	seats	
50	curtains	flowers	
51	bless		
52	either		
53	verse		
54	pasta		
55	anger		
56	four	hours	
57	close	behind	
58	threw	board	
59	mouse	floor	
60	copied	written	
61	weak, feeble		
62	winner, champion		

63 still, motionless
64 close, end
65 fed, eaten

Mixed paper 4

1 15
2 12
3 10
4 13
5 16
6 gain
7 roped
8 tread
9 toils
10 panic
11 RATES — STARE
12 SCALP — CLASP
13 GREAT — GRATE
14 FRAIL — FLAIR
15 STRAP — PARTS
16 feed — eat
17 seek — search
18 cash — money
19 bowl — dish
20 assisting — helping
21 BEST
22 MIST
23 PILL
24 WANT
25 STOP
26 late — music school
27 dog — wall sister
28 athlete — receive medal
29 frogs — caterpillars — butterflies
30 football — park weekends
31 n
32 r
33 y
34 e
35 h
36 SEEN
37 NOSE
38 SANE
39 MOAN
40 ❶❺❷❻
41 UA — RB
42 A3 — b4
43 JQ — LO
44 AC — MO
45 XW — PO
46 STAIR
47 BATHE
48 STICK
49 FLOUR

50 SCARCE
51 LOW
52 OWN
53 NET
54 SEA
55 BAT
56 ROAD
57 SPARE
58 FULL
59 DELAY
60 BUST

61
B	A	S	I	N
A		O		A
N		N		S
J	O	I	N	T
O		C		Y

62
B	I	B	L	E
A		R		Q
T		I		U
C	O	B	R	A
H		E		L

63
S	T	A	F	F
I		Z		A
T	H	U	M	B
E		R		L
S	I	E	V	E

64
P	A	S	T	E
A		W		L
S	O	U	N	D
T		N		E
A	N	G	E	R

65
P	E	T	A	L
A		R		A
C	L	A	M	P
K		D		E
S	H	E	L	L

Mixed paper 5

1 1 3 3 1 2
2 £ + ^ =
3 n k y u
4 TREE
5 O P U
6 DOCK

7 SEEM
8 DEAR
9 COLD
10 SITE
11 p
12 f
13 a
14 m
15 d
16 t
17 p
18 q
19 u
20 s
21 sad, upset
22 stout, plump
23 ready, prepared
24 luck, chance
25 steady, firm
26–30 April A; summer B; Wednesday C; March A; Friday C; May A; Tuesday C; November A; spring B; winter B
31 fur
32 nib
33 a player
34 petals
35 stuffing
36 north
37 east
38 south-east
39 shops
40 post office
41 BORN
42 NEED
43 BARN
44 DARN
45 s u x v
46 love
47 master
48 green
49 grand
50 care
51 wet
52 sweet
53 mad
54 start
55 crowded
56 herself — Maria
57 broken — mended
58 at — in
59 with — or
60 driving — stopped
61 XY
62 OP
63 ZA
64 NQ
65 OR

Bond STRETCH Verbal Reasoning Tests and Papers 9–10 years

ANSWERS

Mixed paper 6

1	church	square
2	garden	across
3	stormy	waves
4	drink	snack
5	clock	three
6	8	16
7	26	16
8	5	33
9	6	5
10	16a	10d
11	CROOK	
12	KNOT	
13	NEST	
14	SINGE	
15	WEARY	
16	A	
17	R	
18	D	

19

F	A	B	L	E
L	■	■	A	■
U	L	T	R	A
F	■	■	G	■
F	O	X	E	S

20

P	O	W	E	R
A	■	■	A	■
R	E	A	R	S
K	■	■	L	■
S	T	A	Y	S

21	WORTH	THROW
22	THESE	SHEET
23	WORSE	SWORE
24	SPORT	PORTS
25	THORN	NORTH
26	worse, better	
27	climb, descend	
28	simple, complicated	
29	shout, whisper	
30	obey, defy	
31	them	
32	seat	
33	then	
34	tour	
35	hear	
36	repair	
37	vanish	
38	simple	
39	attack	
40	horrify	
41	green	
42	box	
43	black	
44	better	
45	under	
46	SANK	
47	3 5 7 6	
48	BASE	
49	5 7 3 4	
50	TAKE	
51	hall	
52	ride	
53	saddle	
54	fare	
55	man	
56	B	
57	E and F	
58	D	
59	4	
60	B	
61	K F G P	
62	LACE	
63	M B U F	
64	U J N F	
65	HOUR	

Mixed paper 7

1	BIRD	
2	HURT	
3	SIDE	
4	GATE	
5	SPUR	
6	finger	waist
7	apple	pear
8	gate	garden
9	bridge	road
10	body	arm
11	14	
12	22	
13	19	
14	B	
15	C	
16	damp	soaking
17	healthy	ailing
18	whole	part
19	Tennis	racquet
20	road	train
21	A	
22	G	
23	D	
24	C	
25	F	
26	CD	LM
27	FH	NP
28	BM	FQ
29	SF	UD
30	BC	DB
31	agree	
32	moan	
33	achieve	
34	peculiar	
35	fib	
36	they	
37	vest	
38	love	
39	herd	
40	vein	
41	leave	depart
42	grow	increase
43	maybe	perhaps
44	glue	paste
45	think	ponder
46	postman	
47	starlight	
48	below	
49	shipwreck	
50	ballroom	
51	p	
52	r	
53	e	
54	g	
55	h	
56	# & * ^	
57	NIPS	
58	@ g 8 4	
59	RENT	
60	U Y C P	
61	DUSK	
62	COME	
63	PONY	
64	TOLL	
65	VAIN	

Mixed paper 8

1	treat	
2	steer	
3	spies	
4	rears	
5	sneer	
6	sack	lawn
7	nave	knit
8	reed	grasp
9	bred	spray
10	sale	scour

11

C	R	U	S	T
O	■	N	■	O
M	E	D	I	A
E	■	E	■	S
S	T	R	U	T

12

S	P	E	A	K
T	■	A	■	E
E	A	G	E	R
E	■	L	■	B
R	E	E	D	S

13	T	
14	E	
15	L	
16	hall	
17	move	
18	chin	
19	lord	
20	wasp	
21	C B M M	
22	R M L C	
23	FIRM	
24	STIR	
25	BEAK	
26	b	
27	f	
28	e	
29	f	
30	c	
31	ROSE	
32	EXIT	
33	TEAM	
34	GOLD	
35	LOOP	
36	future	
37	external	
38	private	
39	closed	
40	rise	
41	HARE	
42	BENT	
43	BURY	
44	WIND	
45	COPE	
46	STEAL	
47	TOAST	
48	TOWER	
49	FREED	
50	DANGER	
51	Bo	
52	Hamish	
53	Sue	
54	sausages	
55	D	
56	redden	blush
57	conceal	hide
58	lost	missing
59	London	Cardiff
60	agile	nimble
61	BP	XM
62	NL	QI
63	OP	ST
64	Yb	Ve
65	po	ON

Give the missing two numbers in the following sequence.

Example   2   4   6   8   <u>10</u>   <u>12</u>

41   13   11   —   —   5   3

42   —   10   15   20   —   30

43   1   15   2   —   —   15

44   2   —   —   32   42   52

45   1   2   4   7   —   —   **5**

Underline the pair of words most opposite in meaning.

Example   cup, mug   coffee, milk   <u>hot, cold</u>

46   before, after   tiny, small   between, in

47   until, therefore   taken, stolen   careful, careless

48   cat, dog   healthy, ill   kind, sort

49   windy, rainy   quickly, slowly   heated, warmed

50   close, near   near, beside   inside, outside   **5**

Find and underline the two words that need to change places for each sentence to make sense.

Example   She went to <u>letter</u> the <u>write</u>.

51   It was morning so hard this raining, we got soaked.

52   Our bear chewed my favourite teddy dog.

53   That vase of table on the flowers is pretty.

54   The old man drove his garage carefully into the car.

55   A fluffy, white sky blew across the blue cloud.   **5**

Choose the word or phrase that makes each sentence true.

Example   A LIBRARY always has (posters, a carpet, <u>books</u>, DVDs, stairs).

56   A CAR always has (a stereo, occupants, a driver, an engine, cloth seats).

57   A BOOK always has (pages, a story, pictures, long words).

58   An ISLAND is always (deserted, surrounded by water, tropical, small).

59 A BIRD always has (a cage, feathers, seed, a tree).

60 A FIRE always has (heat, wood, coal, a chimney, fireworks).

5

Change the first word of the third pair in the same way as the other pairs to give a new word.

Example bind, hind   bare, hare   but, <u>hut</u>

61	tin, tan	rim, ram	hit, _____
62	ran, rook	bit, book	car, _____
63	butter, but	bargain, bar	business, _____
64	hard, hill	bard, bill	ward, _____
65	what, hat	knit, nit	zone, _____

5

Now go to the Progress Chart to record your score!   Total   **65**

Mixed paper 3

The code for STABLES is 1 5 8 4 3 2 1. Decode these into words.

1 3 8 1 1 _____   **2** 4 2 1 5 _____

Encode these words using the same code.

3 TALE _____   **4** EAST _____

Using the same code, decode:

5 3 8 4 2 3. _____

5

Underline the one word in the brackets that will go equally well with both the pairs of words outside the brackets.

Example rush, attack   cost, fee   (price, hasten, strike, <u>charge</u>, money)

6 flatten, press down   print, mark   (tread, parcel, letter, stamp, crush)

7 annexe, extension   fly, limb   (wing, house, feather, plane, arm)

8 metal, unbending   uncrease, straighten   (steel, lead, iron, smooth, heat)

9	planet, constellation	celebrity, personality	(moon, sun, star, galaxy, world)	
10	above, higher than	finished, ended	(on, excessive, dead, beyond, over)	5

Underline the two words, one from each group, that are the most opposite in meaning.

Example   (dawn, <u>early</u>, wake)   (<u>late</u>, stop, sunrise)

11 (laugh, frown, smile)   (talk, complain, cry)

12 (find, fill, file)   (keep, own, lose)

13 (steal, joy, still)   (try, rob, grief)

14 (dash, dot, dull)   (rush, bright, hurry)

15 (border, higher, highest)   (lower, flower, edge)   5

Which one letter can be added to the front of all of these words to make new words?

Example __are   __at   __rate   __all   <u>c</u>

16 __eat   __otter   __ill   __anger   __

17 __ice   __ant   __each   __after   __

18 __angle   __hat   __each   __rue   __

19 __end   __lack   __other   __and   __

20 __pear   __mug   __now   __often   __   5

Fill in the missing letters. The alphabet has been written out to help you.

A B C D E F G H I J K L M N O P Q R S T U V W X Y Z

Example   AB is to CD as PQ is to <u>RS</u>.

21 DF is to HJ as LN is to ___.

22 GM is to FN as PV is to ___.

23 QR is to ST as UV is to ___.

24 MR is to NS as OT is to ___.

25 AZ is to BY as CX is to ___.   5

At a riding stable, there are eight stables in two rows opposite each other. From the information, work out which horse is in each stable.

STABLE BLOCK A

1	2	3	4
BLACK BEAUTY			SHADOW

WALKWAY

5	6	7	8
		TRIGGER	

STABLE BLOCK B

Tommy is in the same row as Trigger but not the same as Crystal.

Captain is next to Secret in the same row. Secret has one of the end stables.

Paloma is unkind to Shadow. They are not in next-door stables.

26 Tommy is in stable number _____.

27 Crystal is in stable number _____.

28 Captain is in stable number _____.

29 Secret is in stable number _____.

30 Paloma is in stable number _____.

5

Find the four-letter word hidden at the end of one word and the beginning of the next word in each sentence. The order of the letters may not be changed.

Example   We had bat<u>s and</u> balls.   <u>sand</u>

31 He wants to be an astronaut when he grows up.   _____

32 Fireworks lit up the dark night sky.   _____

33 She blew out all the candles on her cake.   _____

34 My bicycle is chained to the yard railings.   _____

35 The river burst the far bank, flooding the valley.   _____

5

Rearrange the letters in capitals to make another word. The new word has something to do with the first two words or phrases.

Example   spot   soil   SAINT   <u>STAIN</u>

36   low price   inexpensive   PEACH   _____

37   hot vapour   water droplets   MEATS   _____

38   container   case   TRACE   _____

39   instruct   educate   CHEAT   _____

40   enchant   delight   MARCH   _____   **5**

Remove one letter from the word in capital letters to leave a new word. The meaning of the new word is given in the clue.

Example   AUNT   an insect   <u>ANT</u>

41   PASTE   ended   _____

42   DREAD   not alive   _____

43   CLASP   applaud   _____

44   LEVER   always   _____

45   FOUND   keen on   _____   **5**

Change one word so that the sentence makes sense. Underline the word you are taking out and write your new word on the line.

Example   I waited in line to buy a <u>book</u> to see the film.   <u>ticket</u>

46   Sol slipped on the step and caught down onto the hard ground.   _____

47   At the Olympics, our country won lots of gold presents.   _____

48   After clucking loudly, the hen laid a large table in her nest box.   _____

49   The film had already started as we found our mats in the cinema.   _____

50   He walked into the garden and picked some pretty curtains.   _____   **5**

Underline the one word in each group that **cannot be made** from the letters of the word in capital letters.

Example STATIONERY   stone   tyres   ration   <u>nation</u>   noisy

51	SHAMBLE	lambs	meals	leash	bless	blame
52	WEATHER	there	water	either	threw	wheat
53	DRIVERS	river	verse	sired	drive	diver
54	PASTURE	strap	purse	paste	repast	pasta
55	MANAGES	games	names	manes	sang	anger

◯ 5

Rearrange the muddled words in capital letters so that each sentence makes sense.

Example   There are sixty SNODCES <u>seconds</u> in a UTMINE <u>minute</u>.

56   There are twenty-UROF _____ RSUHO _____ in a day.

57   Please SECOL _____ the door quietly HIBEDN _____ you.

58   The darts player WRETH _____ his dart accurately at the DROBA

_____.

59   The little MSOUE _____ scampered across the ROLOF

_____.

60   We PICODE _____ down what the teacher had WTTENRI

_____.

◯ 5

Underline the pair of words most similar in meaning.

Example   come, go   <u>roams, wanders</u>   fear, fare

61	weak, feeble	delicate, strong	fill, empty
62	winning, losing	fail, pass	winner, champion
63	now, then	up, down	still, motionless
64	far, near	close, end	stop, start
65	bet, beaten	said, sitting	fed, eaten

◯ 5

Mixed paper 4

If m = 6, r = 1, o = 3, e = 2 and f = 5, what are the totals of these words?

1 form _____   2 more _____

3 reef _____   4 room _____

5 offer _____

5

Underline the one word in each group that **can be made** from the letters of the word in capital letters.

Example   CHAMPION   camping   notch   peach   cramp   <u>chimp</u>

6 DANCING   grace   cling   grain   icing   grand

7 DROPPED   roped   prods   error   drops   pedal

8 TRACKED   crack   tread   rakes   darts   cakes

9 FLORIST   stiff   toils   forest   store   relief

10 CAMPING   cramp   image   grain   clamp   panic

5

Underline the two words that are made from the same letters.

Example   TAP   PET   <u>TEA</u>   POT   <u>EAT</u>

11 STRUT   RATES   STARE   STEER   RUSTY

12 PASTE   STRIP   SCARF   SCALP   CLASP

13 GRASP   GREAT   TRADE   GRATE   BUDGE

14 FIERY   FRAIL   FAIRY   RIFLE   FLAIR

15 STRAP   SPARE   PARTS   STAMP   PRISM

5

Underline the two words, one from each group, that are the closest in meaning.

Example   (race, shop, <u>start</u>)   (finish, <u>begin</u>, end)

16 (feed, swallow, fill)   (eat, drink, empty)

17 (seek, entertain, hike)   (keep, fine, search)

18 (card, cash, book)   (money, mine, read)

19 (basket, bowl, spoon)   (knife, dish, box)

20 (assisting, stopping, shopping)   (clipping, helping, hiding)

5

Look at the first group of three words. The word in the middle has been made from the two other words. Complete the second group of three words in the same way, making a new word in the middle of the group.

Example PA<u>IN</u>   INTO   <u>TO</u>OK   ALSO   <u>SOON</u>   ONLY

21 POUR   URGE   GETS   ROBE   _____   STEP

22 CAME   SOME   SOFA   POST   _____   MILK

23 BARD   YARD   DOZY   SILT   _____   LOOP

24 HELP   HELM   PUMA   WAND   _____   CITY

25 CREW   FLOW   FOOL   STEP   _____   SLOT   5

Complete the following sentences by selecting the most sensible word from each group of words given in the brackets. Underline the words selected.

Example The (<u>children</u>, boxes, foxes) carried the (houses, <u>books</u>, steps) home from the (greengrocer, <u>library</u>, factory).

26 On Tuesdays, I am (late, hungry, ill) home as I have a (custard, music, blue) lesson at (school, home, hospital).

27 That fierce (chicken, aeroplane, dog) barked at us over the garden (wall, window, doll) and frightened my little (sister, telephone, spider).

28 At the Olympics, the winning (athlete, boat, horse) climbed onto the podium to (receive, throw, lose) the gold (statue, ring, medal).

29 Tadpoles turn into (cats, frogs, beetles) and (piglets, puppies, caterpillars) turn into (geese, butterflies, chickens).

30 We like to kick a (wall, football, boot) about in the (car, park, traffic) at (weekends, first, them).   5

Find the letter that will end the first word and start the second word.

Example drow (<u>n</u>) ought

31 yaw (__) othing   32 flowe (__) ush   33 sta (__) acht

34 spik (__) ntry   35 ras (__) oney   5

Match the right code to each of the words below.

        MOAN   SANE   SEEN   NOSE
        ❶❺❸❻   ❷❹❺❸   ❸❹❶❻   ❶❻❻❸

36 ❶❻❻❸ _____   37 ❸❹❶❻ _____

34

38 ① ⑤ ③ ⑥ _____   **39** ② ④ ⑤ ③ _____

40 Using the same code, what is the code for SAME?   _____   ◯ 5

Give the two missing pairs of letters and numbers in the following sequences.
The alphabet has been written out for you.

A B C D E F G H I J K L M N O P Q R S T U V W X Y Z

Example	CQ	DP	EQ	FP	GQ	HP
41 WA	VB	—	TB	SA	—
42 —	—	C3	d4	E3	f4
43 HS	IR	—	KP	—	MN
44 —	EG	IK	—	QS	UW
45 ZY	—	VU	TS	RQ	—

◯ 5

Add one letter to the word in capital letters to make a new word. The
meaning of the new word is given in the clue.

Example	PLAN	simple	PLAIN
46	STAR	step	_____
47	BATH	to wash	_____
48	SICK	glue	_____
49	FOUR	ground grain	_____
50	SCARE	rare	_____

◯ 5

Find the three-letter word that can be added to the letters in capitals to make
a new word. The new word will complete the sentence sensibly. Write the
three-letter word.

Example   The cat sprang onto the MO.   USE

51 At a sleepover, we had a PIL fight.   _____

52 We walked D the steep hill together.   _____

53 Our garden has lots of stinging TLES and other weeds.   _____

54 We made sandcastles on our day out at the SIDE.   _____

55 After the rugby match, Simon had a nice, hot H.   _____   ◯ 5

Find a word that is similar in meaning to the word in capital letters and that rhymes with the second word.

Example	CABLE	tyre	<u>WIRE</u>
56	STREET	mode	_____
57	EXTRA	wear	_____
58	COMPLETE	bull	_____
59	HINDER	stay	_____
60	BROKEN	dust	_____

5

Fill in the crosswords so that all the given words are included. You have been given one letter as a clue in each crossword.

61

	■		■	
	■		■	
	■	C	■	

SONIC
JOINT
BASIN
BANJO
NASTY

62

		B		
	■		■	
	■		■	
	■		■	

BATCH
EQUAL
COBRA
BRIBE
BIBLE

63

			F	
	■		■	
	■			

SITES
STAFF
FABLE
SIEVE
AZURE
THUMB

64

	■		■	
	■		■	
		G		

PASTE
PASTA
ELDER
ANGER
SOUND
SWUNG

65

	■		■	
	L			
	■		■	

TRADE
SHELL
LAPEL
PETAL
CLAMP
PACKS

5

Now go to the Progress Chart to record your score!   Total   65

36

1 If the code for SMOOTH is 5 4 3 3 1 2, what is the code
   for TOOTH?   _____

2 If the code for CRIMES is ^ * + £ = @, what is the code
   for MICE?   _____

3 If the code for BROTHER is n g k y u s g, what is the code
   for BOTH?   _____

4 Using the same code, decode y g s s.   _____

5 If the code for YES is Z F T, what is the code for NOT? _____   (5)

Change the first word into the last word by changing one letter at a time and
making a new, different word in the middle.

Example <u>CASE</u>   <u>CASH</u>   LASH

6 LOCK   _____   DECK

7 SEAM   _____   SEEN

8 DEER   _____   DEAF

9 TOLD   _____   COLT

10 BITE   _____   SIZE   (5)

Which one letter can be added to the front of all of these words to make new
words?

Example __are   __at   __rate   __all   <u>c</u>

11 __ear   __each   __ink   __article   __

12 __light   __lower   __air   __ill   __

13 __go   __mble   __float   __cross   __

14 __utter   __ass   __oral   __others   __

15 __airy   __own   __itch   __evil   __   (5)

If p = 2, q = 5, r = 3, s = 10, t = 12 and u = 4, work out the answer to these. Write each answer as a letter.

16 q + r + u = _____

17 t − (pq) = _____

18 (t − r) − u = _____

19 (s ÷ q) × p = _____

20 (p × u) + (q − r) = _____

⬤ 5

Underline the pair of words most similar in meaning.

Example   come, go   <u>roams, wanders</u>   fear, fare

21 quiet, loud   drip, pour   sad, upset

22 stout, plump   thin, fat   odd, even

23 under, above   ready, prepared   leave, lend

24 win, lose   luck, chance   full, empty

25 steady, firm   brave, cowardly   bend, straighten

⬤ 5

Look at these groups of words.

A	B	C
Months	Seasons	Days

Choose the correct group for each of the words below. Write in the letter.

26–30 April __   summer __   Wednesday __   March __   Friday __

May __   Tuesday __   November __   spring __   winter __

⬤ 5

Choose the word or phrase that makes each sentence true.

Example   A LIBRARY always has (posters, a carpet, <u>books</u>, DVDs, stairs).

31 A RABBIT always has (a carrot, a hutch, fur, a warren, babies).

32 A PEN always has (paper, colours, a nib, writing, a cap).

33 A GAME always has (written rules, cheats, balls, captains, a player).

34 A ROSE always has (a smell, petals, sunshine, an arch, a red colour).

35 A PILLOW always has (a bed, stuffing, feathers, a pillowcase, a head).

⬤ 5

Using the map below, select the correct compass points in the questions.

LIBRARY	POST OFFICE
AL'S HOUSE	
SHOPS	DOCTOR'S SURGERY

N
W ← → E
S

36 The library is due _____ from the shops.

37 The post office is due _____ from the library.

38 Which direction does Al go from his house to the doctors' surgery? _____

39 What is south-west from Al's house? _____

40 What is north-east from Al's house? _____ 5

Match the correct code to the words below.

BARN   NEED   DARN   BORN

41 t u s j   _____

42 j v v x   _____

43 t k s j   _____

44 x k s j   _____

45 Using the same code, what is RODE?   _____ 5

Find a word that can be put in front of each of the following words to make new, compound words.

Example	cast	fall	ward	pour	_down_
46	sick	bird	able	less	_____
47	mind	piece	class	fully	_____
48	house	grocer	fly	field	_____
49	father	parent	son	child	_____
50	taker	worn	free	less	_____

5

39

Underline the one word in brackets that is most opposite in meaning to the word in capitals.

Example WIDE   (broad   vague   long   <u>narrow</u>   motorway)

51   FINE   (excellent   bright   wet   hot   cloudless)

52   SOUR   (sharp   bitter   easy   clean   sweet)

53   SANE   (mad   reasonable   funny   sad   bumpy)

54   FINISH   (end   depart   start   belong   ask)

55   DESERTED   (alone   crowded   plain   throng   energetic)   **5**

Find and underline the two words that need to change places for each sentence to make sense.

Example She went to <u>letter</u> the <u>write</u>.

56   The kettle boiled and herself made Maria a cup of tea.

57   The carpenter broken the mended door.

58   We checked at four suitcases in the airport.

59   Would you like salad with vegetables or your steak?

60   The policeman driving the man who was stopped too fast.   **5**

Fill in the missing letters. The alphabet has been written out to help you.

A B C D E F G H I J K L M N O P Q R S T U V W X Y Z

Example AB is to CD as PQ is to <u>RS</u>.

61   AD is to BC as WZ is to ___.   62   CD is to GH as KL is to ___.

63   TU is to VW as XY is to ___.   64   BE is to FI as JM is to ___.

65   HI is to GJ as PQ is to ___.   **5**

Now go to the Progress Chart to record your score!   Total   **65**

Mixed paper 6

Rearrange the muddled words in capital letters so that each sentence makes sense.

Example There are sixty SNODCES <u>seconds</u> in a UTMINE <u>minute</u>.

1   The RCHUCH _____ bells rang out across the QSUREA _____.

2 I saw a fox in the DNEAGR _____ of a house SCROAS

_____ the road.

3 It was YMORTS _____ when we crossed the sea and the VSEWA

_____ were big.

4 We stopped for a RDNIK _____ and a SKNAC _____ halfway
through our journey.

5 The grandfather CKOLC _____ chimed RETHE _____ times. ⬭ 5

Give the two missing numbers and/or letters in the following sequences.

Example	2	4	6	8	<u>10</u>	<u>12</u>
6	4	—	12	—	20	24
7	36	31	—	21	—	11
8	33	—	33	6	—	7
9	20	15	11	8	—	—
10	—	14b	12c	—	8e	6f

⬭ 5

Add one letter to the word in capital letters to make a new word. The
meaning of the new word is given in the clue.

Example	PLAN	simple	<u>PLAIN</u>
11	COOK	a shepherd's staff	_____
12	NOT	a fastening	_____
13	NET	for eggs	_____
14	SING	burn lightly	_____
15	WEAR	tired	_____

⬭ 5

If the letters in the word CRADLE are put into alphabetical order:

16 which comes first? _____

17 which comes last? _____

18 which comes third? _____

⬭ 3

Fill in the crosswords so that all the given words are included. You have been given one letter as a clue in each crossword.

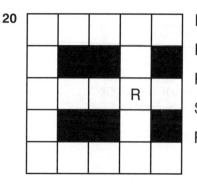

19   LARGE
      ULTRA
      FOXES
      FLUFF
      FABLE

      F

20   REARS
      EARLY
      POWER
      STAYS
      PARKS

      R

2

Underline the two words that are made from the same letters.

Example TAP   PET   <u>TEA</u>   POT   <u>EAT</u>

21 THROB   WORTH   WAIST   THROW   STRAW

22 BIRTH   THESE   SHAME   MATHS   SHEET

23 ROAST   STORE   RESTS   WORSE   SWORE

24 POSTS   TRAPS   SPORT   SPURT   PORTS

25 SHINS   THORN   THINS   NORTH   HANDS

5

Underline the pair of words most opposite in meaning.

Example cup, mug   coffee, milk   <u>hot, cold</u>

26 shabby, worn   worse, better   worry, bother

27 similar, alike   climb, descend   opposite, odd

28 simple, complicated   pain, ache   clear, evident

29 huff, puff   talk, speak   shout, whisper

30 object, protest   light, fluffy   obey, defy

5

Find the four-letter word hidden at the end of one word and the beginning of the next word in each sentence. The order of the letters may not be changed.

Example We had bats <u>and</u> balls.   *sand*

31 We scored four goals in the match.   _____

32 The lighthouse warned ships on the sea that there were rocks nearby.   _____

33 In winter, the days are short and the nights are long. _____

34 Please collect our tickets from the desk. _____

35 The tourists walked slowly through the arch. _____ 〔5〕

Underline the word in the brackets closest in meaning to the word in capitals.

Example UNHAPPY (unkind death laughter <u>sad</u> friendly)

36 MEND (release resort retain repair relay)

37 DISAPPEAR (vanish expect improve find spill)

38 EFFORTLESS (difficult tiring smaller simple pleased)

39 FIGHT (display taunt play bother attack)

40 APPAL (fruit horrify open apply ask) 〔5〕

Underline the one word in the brackets that will go equally well with both the pairs of words outside the brackets.

Example rush, attack cost, fee (price, hasten, strike, <u>charge</u>, money)

41 common land, grassed area emerald, jade (field, olive, green, vegetation, park)

42 container, a confined space punch, hit (slap, pot, box, jar, bottle)

43 ebony, inky dark, no light (brown, purple, black, night, anger)

44 more desirable, effective recovered, well (cured, solved, improve, better, nicer)

45 lower level, lower grade below, beneath (above, higher, inside, through, under) 〔5〕

If the code for BLANKETS is 6 5 7 1 0 2 4 3, work out the following.

46 Decode 3 7 1 0. _____

47 Encode SLAB. _____

48 Decode 6 7 3 2. _____

49 Encode LAST. _____

50 Decode 4 7 0 2. _____ 〔5〕

Change the first word of the third pair in the same way as the other pairs to give a new word.

Example   bind, hind   bare, hare   but, <u>hut</u>

51 catch, call   batch, ball   hatch, _____

52 robe, bore   tale, late   dire, _____

53 port, sort   pane, sane   paddle, _____

54 lantern, tern   shook, hook   fanfare, _____

55 wood, mood   were, mere   wan, _____   5

Six friends have pets. From the information below, answer the questions.

A, B and C have cats. B, D and E have dogs.

A and F have rabbits. B has budgies in the garden in an aviary.

C has chickens and D has guinea pigs.

56 Who has a cat as well as a dog?   _____

57 Which children have only one type of pet?   _____

58 Who has a dog and guinea pigs?   _____

59 How many types of animals do C and D have between them?   _____

60 Who has the most types of animals?   _____   5

The code for CATTLE is D F G G K P.

61 What is the code for LATE?   _____

62 Using the same code, decode K F D P.   _____

A B C D E F G H I J K L M N O P Q R S T U V W X Y Z

If the code for EARLY is F B S M Z, what is the code for:

63 LATE?   _____

64 TIME?   _____

65 Using the same code, decode I P V S.   _____   5

Mixed paper 7

Look at the first group of three words. The word in the middle has been made from the two other words. Complete the second group of three words in the same way, making a new word in the middle of the group.

Example PAIN INTO T<u>OO</u>K   ALSO <u>SOON</u> ONLY

1 HARK   HARP   PING   BIRO   _____   DAMP

2 KING   KISS   FUSS   HUNG   _____   SORT

3 HERE   HOPE   PROW   SOME   _____   DRIP

4 PIES   SOCK   ROCK   FROG   _____   LATE

5 DIES   EDGE   GONE   PERT   _____   URNS   (5

Underline the two words that are the odd ones out in the following group of words.

Example black   <u>king</u>   purple   green   <u>house</u>

6 ear   finger   nose   waist   eye

7 apple   carrot   swede   pear   cabbage

8 gate   tree   flower   garden   weed

9 river   bridge   stream   canal   road

10 paw   hoof   body   foot   arm   (5

If e = 2, a = 1, s = 7, t = 4, f = 5 and r = 3, what are the totals of these words?   (3

11 treat _____   12 staff _____   13 feast _____

Read the first two statements and then underline one of the four options below that must be true.

14 Clowns often perform in circuses. Clowns make people laugh.

    A Circuses tour the country.   B People laugh at clowns in circuses.

    C People don't cry at circuses.   D Clowns are only found in circuses.

15 Today is Friday. It is rainy today.

    A It always rains on Fridays.   B It only rains on Fridays.

    C It can rain on Fridays.   D It never rains on Friday.   (2

Complete the following sentences in the best way by choosing one word from each set of brackets.

Example Tall is to (tree, <u>short</u>, colour) as narrow is to (thin, white, <u>wide</u>).

16 Moist is to (damp, same, brittle) as saturated is to (dry, brave, soaking).

17 Sick is to (unwell, complete, healthy) as well is to (ailing, airing, angry).

18 Entire is to (each, thorough, whole) as partial is to (part, past, full).

19 (Tennis, Riding, Running) is to (racquet, stick, ball) as cricket is to bat.

20 Car is to (passengers, windscreen, road) as (plane, bike, train) is to tracks.

5

In a refrigerated section of a supermarket there are two shelves of goods, one above the other. From the information below, find the correct area for each type of food.

LEFT   TOP   RIGHT

A	B FOREIGN CHEESE	C	D
E YOGURT	F	G	H BUTTER

BOTTOM

The cream is somewhere to the left of the fruit juice but to the right of the yogurt.

The milk is not next to either of the cheeses. It is directly under the fruit juice.

The British cheese is next to the foreign cheese.

The fresh pastry is at one end of the top shelf.

21 British cheese _____   22 milk _____

23 fresh pastry _____   24 fruit juice _____

25 cream _____

5

Give the two missing pairs of letters in the following sequences. The alphabet has been written out for you.

A B C D E F G H I J K L M N O P Q R S T U V W X Y Z

Example CQ   DP   EQ   FP   <u>GQ</u>   <u>HP</u>

26 __   FG   IJ   __   OP   RS

46

27	BD	—	JL	—	RT	VX
28	—	DO	—	HS	JU	LW
29	—	TE	—	VC	WB	XA
30	TC	VB	XC	ZB	—	—	**5**

Underline the word in the brackets closest in meaning to the word in capitals.

Example UNHAPPY (unkind   death   laughter   <u>sad</u>   friendly)

31 CONSENT (conserve   apply   wish   tease   agree)

32 GROAN (moan   hurry   laugh   rusty   price)

33 ATTAIN (strive   think   wonder   achieve   believe)

34 ODD (even   cautious   peculiar   taste   pair)

35 LIE (stand   sit   sleep   free   fib)   **5**

Find the four-letter word hidden at the end of one word and the beginning of the next word in each sentence. The order of the letters may not be changed.

Example We had bat<u>s and</u> balls.   <u>sand</u>

36 The hawk killed the young bird in my garden.   _____

37 Our class bookshelves tumbled down, making us jump.   _____

38 My broken glass shattered all over the floor.   _____

39 Her donkey has a loud bray and huge ears!   _____

40 Polar bears survive in very cold conditions.   _____   **5**

Underline the two words, one from each group, that are the closest in meaning.

Example (race, shop, <u>start</u>)   (finish, <u>begin</u>, end)

41 (leave, entry, far)   (depart, come, near)

42 (grow, decrease, little)   (large, plant, increase)

43 (maybe, bed, in)   (on, bath, perhaps)

44 (bitter, glue, stamp)   (sweet, paste, sugar)

45 (think, behave, like)   (misbehave, distaste, ponder)   **5**

Underline two words, one from each group, that go together to form a new word. The word in the first group always comes first.

Example (hand, <u>green</u>, for)   (light, <u>house</u>, sure)

46 (post, part, pink)   (mail, wing, man)

47 (star, bright, feet)   (stage, strike, light)

48 (be, on, deep)   (high, low, four)

49 (ship, boat, punt)   (float, time, wreck)

50 (take, sore, ball)   (foot, care, room)   **5**

Find the letter that will complete both pairs of words, ending the first word and starting the second. The same letter must be used for both pairs of words.

Example mea (<u>t</u>) able   fi (<u>t</u>) ub

51 stam (__) ick   sto (__) ea

52 ba (__) ash   pur (__) ation

53 purs (__) nd   cur (__) at

54 gan (__) row   sprin (__) rab

55 hig (__) oe   wit (__) elp   **5**

56 If the code for SPRING is $ ^ & * + #, what is the code for GRIP?   _____

57 Using the same code, decode + * ^ $.   _____

58 If the code for WINTER is g 8 4 @ > D, what is the code for TWIN?   _____

59 Using the same code, decode D > 4 @.   _____

A B C D E F G H I J K L M N O P Q R S T U V W X Y Z

Example If the code for CAT is D B U, what is the code for DOG?   <u>E P H</u>

60 If the code for DUCK is F W E M, what is the code for SWAN?   _____   **5**

Change the first word into the last word by changing one letter at a time and making a new, different word in the middle.

Example CASE   <u>CASH</u>   LASH

61 DUST   _____   HUSK

62 COMB   _____   CORE

(48)

63	PUNY	_____	BONY
64	TOOL	_____	TILL
65	VEIN	_____	PAIN

5

Now go to the Progress Chart to record your score!   Total   65

Mixed paper 8

Underline the one word in each group that **cannot be made** from the letters of the word in capital letters.

Example	**STATIONERY**	stone	tyres	ration	<u>nation</u>	noisy
1	CENTRAL	clear	trace	crane	treat	crate
2	WINTERS	stern	swine	steer	rinse	write
3	MAGPIES	image	pages	games	ageism	spies
4	SPEAKER	spear	rakes	parks	pears	rears
5	FINGERS	sneer	grief	singe	grins	fires

5

Move one letter from the first word and add it to the second word to make two new words.

Example	hunt	sip	<u>hut</u>	<u>snip</u>
6	snack	law	_____	_____
7	knave	nit	_____	_____
8	greed	rasp	_____	_____
9	bread	spry	_____	_____
10	scale	sour	_____	_____

5

Fill in the crosswords so that all the given words are included. You have been given one letter as a clue in each crossword.

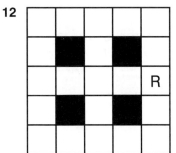

11	MEDIA
	TOAST
	STRUT
	UNDER
	COMES
	CRUST

12	SPEAK
	STEER
	REEDS
	EAGER
	EAGLE
	KERBS

2

49

If all the letters of the word KETTLES are put into alphabetical order, which comes:

13 after S? _____   **14** second? _____

15 in the middle? _____

3

Find the four-letter word hidden at the end of one word and the beginning of the next word in each sentence. The order of the letters may not be changed.

Example   We had bat<u>s and</u> balls.   *sand*

16 He was delighted with all his presents.   _____

17 It rained all day and the stream overflowed.   _____

18 Bats manage to catch insects while they are flying.   _____

19 We had to put words in alphabetical order.   _____

20 Mac was pleased with his test result.   _____

5

A B C D E F G H I J K L M N O P Q R S T U V W X Y Z

Example   If the code for CAT is D B U, what is the code for DOG?   E P H

21 If the code for PARK is Q B S L, what is the code for BALL? _____

22 If the code for ZIPS is X G N Q, what is the code for TONE? _____

23 If the code for DUNE is C T M D, decode E H Q L.   _____

24 If the code for POTS is Q P U T, decode T U J S.   _____

25 If the code for OWLS is L T I P, decode Y B X H.   _____

5

If $d = 2$, $a = 5$, $c = 1$, $b = 12$, $f = 20$ and $e = 3$, work out the answers to these calculations. Write each answer as a letter.

26 $(f \div a) \times e =$ _____   **27** $d + a + c + b =$ _____

28 $(ae) - (cb) =$ _____   **29** $(b \div e) \times a =$ _____

30 $(f - b) - (d + a) =$ _____

5

Look at the first group of three words. The word in the middle has been made from the two other words. Complete the second group of three words in the same way, making a new word in the middle of the group.

Example PA<u>IN</u>   INTO   T<u>OO</u>K   ALSO   SOON   ONLY

31 MADE   DAME   TUNE   SORT   _____   JADE

32 ZIPS   SIDE   EDDY   AXLE   _____   TIDY

50

33	GAME	MEAN	CLAN	RATE	_____	CLAM
34	HOOD	FOOD	FLIP	COLD	_____	GREW
35	ZOOM	MOAN	HAND	POOL	_____	ROPE

Underline the one word in brackets that is most opposite in meaning to the word in capitals.

Example WIDE   (broad   vague   long   <u>narrow</u>   motorway)

36 PAST   (over   done   gone   future   present)

37 INTERNAL   (external   interior   inept   inside   expel)

38 PUBLIC   (popular   crowd   select   brisk   private)

39 OPEN   (ajar   still   closed   quiet   shop)

40 FALL   (tumble   hurt   descend   drop   rise)

Change the first word into the last word by changing one letter at a time and making a new, different word in the middle.

Example CASE   <u>CASH</u>   LASH

41 HARP   _____   MARE

42 BEND   _____   BELT

43 FURY   _____   BUSY

44 KIND   _____   WAND

45 CAPE   _____   COPY

Rearrange the letters in capitals to make another word. The new word has something to do with the first two words or phrases.

Example spot   soil   SAINT   <u>STAIN</u>

46 pinch   take   LEAST   _____

47 to brown   browned bread   STOAT   _____

48 rise over   tall building   WROTE   _____

49 released   set loose   DEFER   _____

50 hazard   peril   GARDEN   _____

51

Six children are waiting in line for lunch.

Malek is at one end of the queue and Suki is third in line.

Hamish and Bo have 3 people between them.

Corinne stands next to and between Sue and Hamish.

51 Who stands behind Malek? _____

52 Who is last in line? _____

53 Who is fourth in line? _____

A and B like curry, C likes sausages but not curry. D likes lasagne and sausages. E only likes sausages.

54 Which is the most popular food? _____

55 Which person likes the most types of food? _____ **5**

Underline the two words in each line that are most similar in type or meaning.

Example <u>dear</u>   pleasant   poor   extravagant   <u>expensive</u>

56 whiten   redden   colouring   crayon   blush

57 strike   conceal   compare   hide   catch

58 lost   found   fiend   here   missing

59 London   Cardiff   Wednesday   winter   leaves

60 quick   slow   agile   nimble   careful **5**

Give the two missing pairs of letters in the following sequences. The alphabet has been written out for you.

A B C D E F G H I J K L M N O P Q R S T U V W X Y Z

Example CQ   DP   EQ   FP   <u>GQ</u>   <u>HP</u>

61 __   XO   BN   __   BL   XK

62 MM   __   OK   PJ   __   RH

63 __   QR   __   UV   WX   YZ

64 Za   __   Xc   Wd   __   Uf

65 ts   SR   rq   QP   __   __ **5**

Now go to the Progress Chart to record your score!   Total **65**